🌺 *Gardens from Garbage* 🌺

Judith F. Handelsman

Gardens FROM GARBAGE

How to grow indoor plants from recycled kitchen scraps

Illustrated by Anne Canevari Green
The Millbrook Press · Brookfield, Connecticut

Published by The Millbrook Press
2 Old New Milford Road
Brookfield, Connecticut 06804

Library of Congress Cataloging-in-Publication Data

Handelsman, Judith F., 1948–
Gardens from garbage : how to grow plants from recycled kitchen
scraps / Judith F. Handelsman.
p.   cm.
Includes bibliographical references and index.

Summary: Provides instructions for growing houseplants from pieces
of potatoes, corn, watermelons, and other kitchen scraps.
ISBN 1-56294-229-8 (lib. bdg.)   ISBN 1-56294-843-1 (pbk.)
1. Vegetable gardening—Juvenile literature.   2. Indoor gardening—
Juvenile literature.   3. Vegetables—Propagation—Juvenile
literature.   4. Fruit-culture—Juvenile literature.   5. Fruit—
Propagation—Juvenile literature.   6. Recycling (Waste, etc.)—
Juvenile literature.   [1. Vegetable gardening.   2. Indoor
gardening.   3. Recycling (Waste)]   I. Title.   II. Green, Anne
Canevari, ill.
SB324.5.H35   1993
635′.048—dc20   92-9146   CIP   AC

❧ *Contents* ❧

To Rhoda Blumberg

❧ *Introduction* ❧

Because of the way we live and the rapid growth of the earth's population, the amount of garbage on our planet has increased. We are now learning to clean up our world by *recycling* aluminum cans, glass bottles, newspapers, plastics, and many other items we used to throw away.

You can find a way to help the earth right in your own kitchen by using leftover fruits and vegetables to grow new plants. Not only will you be recycling, but you will also be growing beautiful houseplants—turning kitchen garbage into an indoor garden.

Plants improve the air quality of your home by giving off *oxygen*. Perhaps this is why we seem to breathe more easily and feel more peaceful in a park than on a city street. Even a few houseplants can help the quality of your home environment by supplying oxygen and adding beauty.

By planting a kitchen garden you can help both the larger environment and your own living space. You can enjoy a creative project, decorate your room, and recycle garbage at the same time.

* * *

When I was in fourth grade, I planted pumpkin seeds from a jack-o'-lantern. In about two weeks, a tiny *sprout* appeared. I loved watching that plant grow and seeing the cycle of life in action. As I have gotten older, I am still happiest when I am gardening. This book is a way for me to share my love of plants and the magic of gardening.

Anyone can experience this magic. To be a gardener you don't have to own land or spend money. In every kitchen garbage bin there is a garden waiting to be planted. After you read this book, your motto can be, "Don't throw it, grow it!"

🐦 *Starting Your Indoor Garden* 🐦

No matter which projects you choose to do in this book, there are certain steps that need to be taken when planting and caring for all types of plants. It is a good idea to turn back to this section and review these steps every time you begin a new project.

GENERAL PLANTING INSTRUCTIONS

You can use any kind of container—clay, plastic, or ceramic. Better yet, recycle coffee tins, milk cartons, and large yogurt or cottage cheese containers for use as planters.

Label your container with the name of the seed and the date you planted it, so that you will know what you have planted and when.

Use a packaged houseplant soil mixture.

Place a few small rocks over the holes in the bottom of the pot so that the soil does not get washed out when the water drains.

When filling the container, pack the soil down lightly.

To plant most seeds: using your fingers, poke holes in the soil about ½ inch (about 1 centimeter) deep. Drop one seed in each hole and cover with soil. You can plant several seeds in each pot. Water well.

Be patient with your seeds. *Germination* (the time it takes to grow) depends on many things: the type of seed and how much light, water, and warmth it needs.

Seeds can take anywhere from a few days to a few months to sprout. If your seed doesn't germinate right away, don't throw the project away. Take care of it and wait. You may have a "late bloomer" in your pot. Sometimes these plants turn out to be healthier, bigger, and more beautiful than the ones that got off to a fast start.

To start plants from materials other than seeds, such as vegetable and fruit parts, turn to the directions given for the individual projects in this book.

COME BACK AND SEE ME IN A MONTH!

TAKING CARE OF
YOUR NEW PLANTS

All houseplants need a room temperature of 55°F (13°C) or warmer.

You can't water too much at one time if you have good *drainage*, but you can water too often. Allow a plant to dry out before you water it again, unless you have specific instructions to keep the plant wet. Test for dryness by sticking your finger into the soil. Remember, the more sun a plant gets, the more water it needs.

Plants enjoy moisture. This is one reason why they grow so well in the kitchen, where steam and running water add *humidity* to the air. You can give your plants extra moisture by spritzing them with water from a plant sprayer a few times a day.

Most vegetables need direct sun. Some, such as yams and avocados, can survive in a north window, where there is light but no direct sun. Don't give up if you don't have a sunny window. You can put your sun-loving plants under special plant-growing lights you can buy in hardware stores or garden centers. Plants need to be within 6 to 10 inches (15 to 25 centimeters) of the lights.

As your plants grow, they may need to be *transplanted* (moved to a new, bigger pot). This is sometimes necessary because plants grow too big and become *top-heavy*. Or the *roots* can grow until they fill the pot and the plant becomes *root bound*.

To transplant: fill the new container halfway with soil. Carefully remove the plant, including the *rootball* (the roots with dirt clinging to them). Set the plant in the half-filled pot. Hold it with one hand and lightly pack soil around it until you fill up the pot to within 1 inch (2.5 centimeters) of the top. The plant should be firmly set and standing up straight in the center of the container. Put the container in the sink and fill it with water. Watch the water drain out completely; then fill and drain again three or four times. This way you can be sure all the dry spots get wet.

❧ *Indoor Projects You Can Do* ❧

The following projects are easy to do. Some show results faster than others. After you try a few, see which types of plants you like to grow best.

Gardening is creative and a lot of fun. There is no one "right way" to do it. Once you know the basics, experiment. If you make a mistake, think of it as a way to learn something new.

It's fun to keep a special notebook recording the growth of your projects. Date all your entries so that you can follow your garden's progress. Write about what you see, what you do, what you learn, and how you feel about it. If you like to draw, your plant notebook is a good place to use your talent.

Your goal is to grow attractive indoor plants from scraps or seeds that are usually tossed out in the garbage. Do not expect to harvest fruits or vegetables. However, you can eat some of the plants you grow, and this book will tell you which ones. Be sure to eat only those specified, because the leaves of some plants can be poisonous.

GARLIC

A bulb of garlic is made up of several cloves, each of which can be separated and planted. About a week after you have planted a clove, expect a green stem to sprout from its top. This smells and tastes

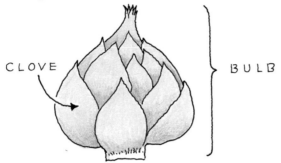

CLOVE   BULB

just like garlic. As the stem grows, you can snip it and add it to salads or spaghetti sauce. More will grow, so enjoy your fresh garlic shoots often.

To plant garlic:

Prepare your container. Separate garlic cloves, carefully removing one clove at a time. Place the clove in the soil with the pointed side sticking up about ½ inch (1 centimeter) above the soil. Plant at least six to eight cloves. Water well and place the pot in direct sun.

The builders of the ancient pyramids in Egypt ate lots of raw garlic. They believed it gave them strength. When the workers were building the great pyramid of Cheops, they went on strike and refused to work until the king collected enough garlic to satisfy them. There is an inscription in Egyptian characters on the pyramid that records the total amount of garlic, onions, and radishes the builders ate. Inscriptions on the pyramids were usually only for things of religious importance. Garlic must have been sacred to the Egyptians.

Six perfectly preserved dried bulbs of garlic were discovered in the tomb of King Tutankhamen. These were found among gold and lapis lazuli, a blue stone that the Egyptians held sacred.

PINEAPPLES

The crown of a pineapple—the prickly, pointed part at the top—can be planted. Pineapples look especially attractive in clay pots. The plant won't bear fruit, but if you keep it in a warm, sunny window, it might produce a pretty blue flower.

You can tell if a pineapple is ready to be eaten if it smells sweet and the top leaves are easy to pull out. When you cut up your pineapple, remove the crown first, leaving about 1 inch (2.5 centimeters) of fruit attached. (Be careful not to hurt your fingers on the spines.)

To plant a pineapple crown:

Prepare your container (make sure it is wide enough to hold the crown). Cover the fruit portion of the pineapple with soil, exposing only the green crown. Water it well, so that the soil is moist but not muddy. Place the container in a warm, sunny spot.

Columbus brought pineapples to Europe from the Caribbean islands in 1493. The Spaniards called it "piña" because it was shaped like a pine cone. To the native Caribbeans, the pineapple was a symbol of hospitality. If they placed it at the entrance to their village, the Spaniards knew it was a sign of welcome. This custom later became popular in Europe, and the British brought it to the American colonies. In North Carolina, Virginia, and New England, the colonists carved the "hospitality fruit" on gateposts, doorways, and furniture as a symbol of welcome and friendship.

The Earl of Dunsmore was a rich man who lived in Scotland in the 1700s. In honor of the first pineapple ever grown in Scotland (in a greenhouse), *he hired the finest architects and masons to build a stone house shaped like a pineapple. It was 40 feet (12 meters) high! The earl used his pineapple palace as a special place to give dinner parties, where, of course, pineapple was served.*

WHITE POTATOES

The leaves of potato plants have a rich, dark green color. The plants are sturdy, attractive, and fast growing. They will not produce potatoes, but you might get some flowers. **Do not eat** any part of your potato plants. They belong to the *nightshade* family and can be poisonous.

When planning your potato project, choose potatoes with lots of "eyes." These are the parts that sprout. Supermarket potatoes are often sprayed with a substance to keep them from sprouting. Since you want your potatoes to sprout, scrub them with a brush and warm running water. Pat the potatoes dry and put them aside. After about a week (depending on how old the potatoes were when you bought them), the potato "eyes" will begin to sprout.

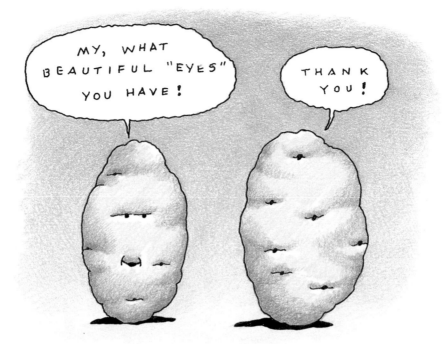

To plant white potatoes:

Cut the sprouted potatoes into pieces, making sure each piece has at least one sprout. Plant the sections in a prepared container about 1 inch (2.5 centimeters) deep. You can plant them together (leave 1 inch or 2.5 centimeters, between the pieces), or place each in a separate pot. Water well and set the container in a sunny window. In less than a week, the sprouts will break through the soil. Test often for dryness by poking your fingers down about an inch into the soil. If it feels dry, water well.

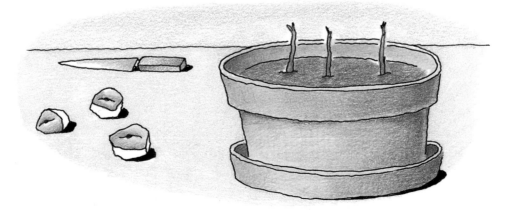

The Incas of South America used potatoes for thousands of years, since they found them growing wild high in the Andes mountains. These native South Americans were the first to make instant mashed potatoes. They did this by stamping on the potatoes to remove all their moisture. Then they dried them in the cold Andes air. Eventually, they got a white powder. When they wanted to eat mashed potatoes, they added boiling water, a little salt, butter, and spices and had a delicious treat.

When the Spanish soldiers, under Francisco Pizarro, took over Peru and destroyed the empire of the Incas in 1532, they discovered potatoes. They took them back on their ships to Europe. The English colonists brought potatoes to Jamestown and Plymouth, but the colonists fed them to their animals. They believed potatoes were poisonous to humans and would cause leprosy and other dreaded diseases.

CITRUS FRUITS

Oranges, lemons, grapefruits, limes, and tangerines are all citrus fruits. Their seeds are easy to sprout and will eventually grow to become small trees. As the tree grows bigger, you must transplant it into larger and larger pots, because it needs plenty of space to grow.

If you have lots of sun and warmth (and luck), flowers may bloom and your tree may even bear fruit indoors. But you also need lots of patience—it can take a citrus tree grown from a seed as long as 15 years to bear fruit! In the meantime, you can enjoy your lovely indoor tree.

Citrus leaves are special. If you rub them between your fingers, you can smell their fresh, lemony fragrance. The leaves of all citrus fruits contain d-limonene, which makes them smell like lemon.

To plant citrus seeds:

Rinse the seeds in warm water and soak them overnight. Prepare your planting container and plant each seed ½ inch (1 centimeter) deep. Leave one inch (2.5 centimeters) between the seeds so that they have room to grow. Water the soil well and keep it moist. The seeds may take a month or more to sprout, but don't give up. Citrus plants need to be placed in the sunniest, warmest spot in your house for best results. As your plants grow, *pinch* back the tips of new growth to help them become bushy.

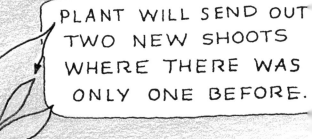

King George III of England grew oranges at his palace in Kew, near London, in a building called an orangery. The orangery was built of brick, had very tall glass windows, and was heated by steam pipes. Inside, orange trees were planted in huge tubs on wheels. During the summer, the royal gardeners wheeled the trees out into the sunshine. In the fall, they wheeled them back into the orangery to keep them warm.

Large-scale commercial orange growing began when Florida became part of the United States in 1821. Today, the principal orange-growing states are Florida, Texas, and California.

CORN

Take your pick. You can plant dried popcorn kernels, or you can plant some fresh corn kernels you have dried yourself. Either way, you will get a hardy houseplant with big, shiny leaves. If you decide to plant fresh corn, you will need to dry the kernels thoroughly on newspaper for several days before planting them. If you don't, they will rot in the soil.

To plant corn:

Cut off a piece of corncob and set it out to dry on newspaper. After a few days, when the corn is completely dry, pick off some kernels. In a prepared pot of soil, make holes about 1 inch (2.5 centimeters) deep and drop in the corn kernels. Cover them with soil and water well. Put the planter in a sunny spot. (If you plant corn in fall or winter, you will need to place it under a growing light.) Check the container each day so that you can keep the soil moist but not soggy. Within two weeks, you should see sprouts.

Corn grows quickly. You may want to transplant the sprouts to separate pots. This will allow the corn plants to grow bigger and stronger. When a plant begins to lean toward the sun, turn it in the other direction so that it won't become lopsided.

North American Indians grew corn for thousands of years before the Europeans arrived. Native Americans treasured corn as a sacred gift from their gods and called it "our mother, our life." Corn was essential to all parts of the Indians' lives, including religious beliefs, customs, and rituals.

By the time Columbus arrived in the New World, the Indians knew how to grow various types of corn in many sizes and colors. Some ears had kernels as large as quarters. Corn came in a variety and mixture of colors—red, yellow, white, blue, brown, gray, and black.

Captain John Smith's letters say that the colonists of Jamestown, Virginia, would have starved in 1607 if the generous Indians had not shared their corn, beans, and squashes with them. Corn was so important in pioneer America that colonists often used it to pay their rent, debts, and taxes.

Popcorn may be the oldest American snack. Native Americans grew it and taught the colonists how to pop it. According to some accounts, Chief Massasoit and his brother Quadquing gave a batch of popcorn to everyone at the end of the first Thanksgiving dinner.

SQUASHES

There are many kinds of squashes. Some, such as zucchini, yellow crookneck, and patty pan, grow in summer. Others, such as acorn and butternut, are harvested in fall and winter. Cucumbers, melons, and pumpkins are familiar members of the squash family. Squash seeds will not produce vegetables indoors, but you will get vines and sometimes yellow trumpet-like flowers, which can be added to salads for color and flavor. If you attach squash vines to a string, you can trail them across walls and windows.

To plant squash seeds:

Put squash seeds in a strainer and rinse them under warm running water. Dry the seeds overnight on newspaper. Make a mound in the soil in your container. Set three to five seeds in the mound about 1 inch (2.5 centimeters) deep. Water well and place the container in a warm place, such as a sunny window. Squash seeds need to be very warm to germinate. Keep the soil moist. You can expect the seeds to germinate in a week to ten days.

Squashes played an important part in the spiritual life of Native Americans. Several tribes used them in their religious rituals. The Indians carved the hard outer shells of gourds (a relative of squash) to make masks for sacred dances.

In South America, one type of squash had such a hard outer shell that the Indians used it as a cooking pot. Then they ate the pot when the food inside it was gone!

BEANS

There are two kinds of projects you can do with beans: you can sprout them for eating in salads, or you can plant them in soil to grow houseplants.

To sprout beans:

For the best flavor, choose garbanzo, adzuki, mung, or whole peas (split peas won't sprout).

Soak each variety of bean overnight in a separate jar. Pour off the soaking water and rinse again. Cover each jar with a piece of cheesecloth or panty hose and fasten with a rubber band so that the beans won't fall out. In the morning and evening, rinse the beans thoroughly.

Between rinsings, tilt the jar in the kitchen dish rack (see illustration on facing page). This allows the jar to drain thoroughly so that the beans don't rot. In two to four days, white sprouts will emerge from your beans.

Eat the beans when the sprouts are very short. They are fresher and more *nutritious* then. However, some people like the flavor of beans when they are mature. Try them both ways. Store the bean sprouts in the refrigerator. This stops their growth. Sprouted beans are a great source of protein and add crunchiness and flavor to salads.

To plant beans in soil:

Select from a wide variety of beans: lima, garbanzo, kidney, mung, and pinto. They all make attractive houseplants. Use a strainer to wash the beans under warm running water. Soak them overnight to soften their hard outer skin, and drain well. In a prepared container, make a hole or mound in the soil and plant the beans 1 inch (2.5 centimeters) deep. Water well. Place your container in a sunny window. Keep the soil moist and watch for the sprouts to break through the surface.

Native Americans ate beans, corn, and squashes together. They planted all three in the same mound. The Iroquois called them "the three inseparable sisters."

In Narraganset Indian legend, a crow brought beans and corn to the Native Americans. In one ear the crow held a kernel of corn, and in the other, a bean. In gratitude and respect, a Narraganset would never scare away a crow from the corn or bean crops.

In the Massachusetts Bay Colony, beans were used to vote in elections. A white bean meant a yes for the candidate. A black bean meant no.

LENTILS

Lentils are part of a food group called *legumes*. Peas and beans are in the legume family, and like beans and peas, lentils can be sprouted for eating or planted in soil for a pretty houseplant. Lentils are tasty in salads and high in protein. They come in different colors—brown, pink, and yellow. The pink ones sprout the fastest. They germinate in one day! If you look at them closely, you will see the beginning of a sprout. Pink lentils, when sprouted, add good flavor and attractive color to salads.

To sprout lentils:

Soak about three tablespoons of dried lentils overnight in a jar of water. After soaking, the lentils swell. It will seem as if they have multiplied. Drain the water out. Rinse the lentils once in the morning and once at night. Fasten cheesecloth or panty hose with a rubber band over the top of the jar. This will keep the lentils from falling out as you rinse them. Tilt the jar against the kitchen dish rack so that the lentils drain thoroughly. In a day or two you will see a tiny white sprout sticking its head out from the crack in the lentil. Eat lentils when they have just sprouted. They are freshest then and have the most food value.

To plant lentils in soil:

Soak overnight and drain. Poke holes about 1 inch (2.5 centimeters) deep into the soil and drop the lentils in. Cover with soil. Within about a week the seed will germinate and vines will begin to grow.

In ancient Rome, practicing Christianity was forbidden. Many Christians met in a secret underground meeting place called the Catacombs. The Christians wanted to have living plants for their altars on holy days. They discovered that lentils would sprout in the dark. It became customary each year for them to plant lentils in clay pots ten days before Easter so that they would have plants for Easter Sunday.

WHEAT BERRIES

Wheat berries are not common in kitchens today. Before packaged flour existed, cooks had to grind wheat berries to make flour for bread, cakes, and cookies. Today, you can buy wheat berries in health food stores.

Wheat berries are exciting to grow. They make the most dramatic show in your kitchen garden. In less than a week after you plant the berries, a thick carpet of grass will appear in your container. Wheat grass is a bright, electric green and grows so fast that sometimes it almost seems to be moving! It grows about 8 inches (20 centimeters) tall before the blades begin to bend and fall over. Wheat grass grows so easily and looks so attractive that it is tempting to plant containers of it all over the house. Some people drink juice made from wheat grass because they believe it keeps them healthy. Wheat grass is edible.

To plant wheat berries:

Fill a wide pot or flat with soil. Spread wheat berries across the top. Soak well. Wheat grass grows with just a little sun. Check the soil every day to make sure that it is moist. Then watch the plants take off!

A gram of wheat stores many of the carbohydrates, fats, proteins, vitamins, and minerals that the human body needs. Whole wheat bread, made from unprocessed flour, is more nutritious than bread made from processed flour. Unprocessed means that no part of the wheat grain is removed.

SUNFLOWER SEEDS

You can plant sunflower seeds for a tall, leafy houseplant (your plant will not produce flowers indoors), or you can sprout them for eating. Sunflower sprouts have a delicious nutty flavor. When planting or sprouting, always use raw sunflower seeds; roasted or salted seeds will not sprout.

To sprout sunflower seeds:

Place the seeds on top of the soil in your container and cover with a double layer of newspaper. Water the seeds through the paper. Place the container in a sunny window, and check often to be sure the newspaper stays wet. In a few days take a peek under the paper. You will see that your seeds have begun to germinate. After they grow to about 1 inch (2.5 centimeters), uncover them and allow the sun to shine on the leaves. The sprouts will turn green and begin to grow quickly. Snip the sprouts with a scissors before the opening of the second set of leaves (see illustration). Rinse the sprouts and pat them dry with paper towels before adding them to a salad or sandwich. They are sweet and crunchy.

To plant sunflower seeds in soil:

Soak unshelled seeds overnight. Place the seeds 1½ inches (about 4 centimeters) deep in a container. Keep them moist. In about two weeks the seeds will sprout. Sunflower plants grow very large and need to be transplanted to larger and larger containers.

Native Americans grew sunflowers for their seeds. They ground these, as they did corn, into meal for baking.

TOMATOES

Tomato plants need to be kept warm all the time. If you have direct sun, you may get tomatoes from your indoor plants. Watch for small, yellow, star-like flowers. After they appear, baby tomatoes develop. If you don't have direct sun, tomato *foliage* will grow in indirect light, but the plants will not produce flowers or fruit. Tomatoes, like potatoes, are members of the nightshade family. **Do not eat** their leaves.

To plant tomatoes:

Wash the tiny seeds in a fine strainer under warm running water. Dry overnight on newspaper. In a prepared container, plant about a dozen seeds just below the surface of the soil. Cover with a thin layer of soil and water well. Keep moist. In about three weeks you should see sprouts. As your tomato plants grow, thin out the weak, skinny ones because they compete for nutrients with the stronger plants. You will need to transplant each healthy *seedling* into its own pot to give it enough room to grow. Tomato plants can become very large. Remember, they don't like cold, so keep them out of drafts.

The Spanish conquerors discovered tomatoes in South America in the 1500s and brought them back to Europe. The colonists brought the seeds to America. But for a long time, the people of North America and in parts of Europe refused to eat tomatoes because they believed they were poisonous. Instead, they grew them in their flower gardens. They used to cut the plants with the fat little red fruits and arrange them in vases in their homes.

Thomas Jefferson was a great experimenter on his farm in Virginia. He planted tomatoes for food in 1781 and was one of the first Americans to eat them. Not many people followed his example. Until the middle of the 1800s, most Americans were afraid tomatoes would make them sick.

ROOT VEGETABLES

Carrots, beets, radishes, turnips, and parsnips are *root vegetables*. The tops of these vegetables are easy to grow. They make pretty houseplants because of the beauty of their foliage. You can grow them on pebbles in water, or, if you want a longer-lasting plant, you can grow them in soil. Carrots and beets give the best results of all the root vegetables when grown on pebbles in water, but you can try others.

To grow root vegetables on pebbles:

Cut the tops off several beets and carrots (choose the biggest, fattest ones), leaving 1 inch (2.5 centimeters) of vegetable on each. If the vegetables have any green on top, cut this off completely. Fill a deep dish or pie plate (without holes) with pebbles to 1 inch (2.5 centimeters) from the top. Place the carrot and beet pieces on top of the pebbles with the cut side down. Arrange the rocks so that the vegetable pieces stand up straight. Add water until it covers the bottoms of the vegetable pieces. Make sure the vegetables are sitting in water but are not completely covered. Do not place the dish in direct sun. Check the water every day to make sure the bottoms of the vegetables are always touching the water. Without water they shrivel. Within a week, sprouts will appear. You will see new growth every day. Your arrangement will last about one month.

To plant root vegetables in soil:

Choose firm, fresh vegetables for best results. Using a stiff brush, wash the vegetable well under running water. Pat dry and cut off any greens on top, but use the **whole** vegetable.

Prepare your planter according to basic directions. Make a hole big enough for the vegetable in the soil. Place the vegetable, root end down, in the hole and cover so that about 1 inch (2.5 centimeters) is showing above the soil. Soak well. Place the planter in a sunny window and check the soil frequently so that it doesn't dry out.

In the 1600s in France, beets became a common vegetable in everyone's garden. French chefs boiled beets and then cut out little red stars, moons, and dancing figures to decorate large platters for special banquets.

Ladies of the court of King James I of England wore carrot leaves on their hats and in their hair.

YAMS

You can grow a very attractive and unusual vine from yams. The younger vines are a rich purple color. As they grow longer, they become a bright green. The vines grow very fast. Yams do best when grown in a glass jar filled with water.

To grow a yam vine in water:

Choose a long, skinny yam for your project. Scrub it under warm running water with a brush. Cut off one end of the yam and stick four toothpicks around the middle so that it can sit easily in a jar full of water. The cut side of the yam should be in the water and the pointed side above (see illustration). Place the jar in light but not direct sun. About a week after planting, you may see white, stringy roots growing from the bottom of the yam. A little later, watch for

purplish leaves sprouting from the top. Keep the jar filled with water. If the water gets cloudy, pour it out and refill.

After the yam plant has been growing for a while, you may have to switch it to a larger jar because the vines become heavy and the roots dense.

Some African yams are so big that you would need a wheelbarrow to carry them home. In Asia, it is not unusual for a yam to weigh as much as 30 or 40 pounds (13.5 or 18 kilograms). South Pacific yams sometimes weigh 100 pounds (45 kilograms)!

AVOCADOS

You can grow an avocado tree that will become 6 feet (almost 2 meters) high from a seed that you might have thrown away. It will not bear fruit indoors. However, you can have a healthy, attractive houseplant. Growing an avocado plant is done in two steps: sprouting in water and then planting in soil.

To sprout an avocado seed:

Avocado seeds grow at different rates, so start three or four at a time. Wash the seeds and let them dry overnight. Peel off the brown outer skin. Some of the smaller seeds are difficult to peel. If the skin tears, don't use the seed.

Stick toothpicks in the seed and place it in a jar of water, flat side down and pointed side up. Store the jar in a dark place, such as a closet or kitchen cabinet. Make sure the jar is filled to the very top with water. The roots must always be in water.

INSERT FOUR TOOTHPICKS TO HOLD PIT

White roots grow out of the bottom of the seed, and the stem rises from the top. When the stem is about 6 inches (15 centimeters) long, use a sharp knife to cut it back to half its size. This will strengthen the plant and help the roots to grow.

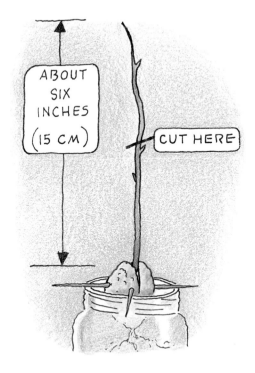

After you cut the stem, put the plant back in the dark and wait another few weeks. Remember to keep the jar filled with water. The roots will thicken, and a new stem will grow from the spot where you cut the old one (see the illustration). When the new stem has grown to 6 inches (15 centimeters), bring it out into the light. The leaves will turn green. (In the dark they stay yellow.)

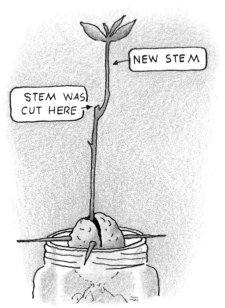

To plant the sprouted seed in soil:

Gently remove your sprouted seed from its glass container. Be very careful not to damage the roots. In a prepared container, make a hole deep enough to hold the roots. Gently fill with soil, but be sure the top inch of the seed shows above the soil. Water the plant well. Repeat whenever the soil dries out.

When new leaves grow at the tips of stems, pinch them off (see illustration). If you allow the avocado plant to grow tall and skinny, with just a few leaves on the top, it will always look like a telephone pole. Pinching the leaves will help the plant branch out and become bushy. For every two new leaves you pinch, four will grow in their place. As your avocado tree gets bigger, you may have to stake it with a stick. If you see roots growing out the hole in the bottom of the pot, it's time to transplant. Your avocado tree may also grow so big that it becomes top-heavy, another reason to transplant.

Incan, Mayan, and Aztec Indians cultivated avocado trees, which originally grew wild. In the court of Montezuma, the Aztec king who ruled in the 1500s, guacamole was served. This Mexican dish, made from mashed avocado, peppers, tomatoes, and onions, is still a favorite snack today.

WATERMELONS

Watermelon seeds won't produce watermelons indoors, but you will get attractive vines. The black seeds found in watermelons are best for planting. Watermelon sprouts are fun to watch. They grow quickly and are very strong. Give them space; they love to spread.

After your success with watermelons, try other melon plants, such as cantaloupes and honeydews.

To plant watermelon seeds:

Wash the seeds and dry them overnight on newspaper. Place the seeds in a prepared planter of soil 1 inch (2.5 centimeters) apart and cover them with ½ inch (1 centimeter) of soil. Or make a small mound and place five seeds ½ inch (1 centimeter) deep in the soil. Cover with a thin layer of soil. Some watermelon seeds sprout sooner than others. Be patient. They almost all come up eventually. Water well and keep the container constantly moist. You may have to water the planter every day, especially if your house is hot or dry. Do not let the soil get muddy.

Sun is very important to watermelon plants. Without it they get skinny and leggy, with few leaves and long vines. The "first leaves" (*cotyledons*) are smooth and oval. The second set are the "true leaves." They are fuzzy and jagged.

Watermelon seeds are a favorite snack in China. In ancient times the Chinese grew watermelons just for their seeds. They hardly ever ate the juicy fruit we love. Watermelons originated in Africa. Watermelon seeds were found in the ancient Egyptian tombs.

APPLES

The next time you eat an apple, save the seeds for growing. You can grow an apple tree right in your own home. It will not bear fruit indoors, but it will reward your patience and care with its lovely green presence. It is important to start many apple seeds at once, because only a few may sprout. Experiment with different kinds of apples to discover which ones are easiest to grow.

To plant apple seeds:

Soak the seeds overnight. Press six to twelve into the soil just below the surface. Add a thin layer of soil. The seeds tend to move around when they are watered. Be sure they have enough soil to keep them in place. Water well. If you plant the seeds in winter, you can place a plastic bag over the top of the pot to help the seeds germinate. This will make the environment warm and humid, like that of a greenhouse.

Apples were a favorite fruit of the English settlers in America. They brought the trees from England on their ships. Even though they were careful not to waste their water, they always watered the apple trees. One can imagine how important the fruit was to them.

Johnny Appleseed, the folk hero of American history, was a real person named John Chapman. He planted apple seeds wherever he went. He collected these seeds from the crushed pulp of pressed apples at Pennsylvania cider mills. From 1797 until he died in 1845, he traveled out west, giving or selling little bags of seeds to everyone he met. Johnny journeyed from the Allegheny Mountains to Iowa, Illinois, Indiana, and Ohio establishing apple orchards.

Once you have done some of the projects in this book, you will have had the satisfaction of seeing garbage become beautiful. It is magical to take kitchen scraps such as seeds and parts of fruits and vegetables and help them grow into lovely, healthy houseplants. Each fruit and vegetable, each seed, is a gift. Hiding within it is a surprise: the gift of life that can become visible with just a little help from you.

🐌 *Glossary* 🐌

Cotyledons—The first set of leaves that grow from a seed. These leaves look different from the next set of leaves, called "true leaves."

Drainage—Pouring out or emptying of water.

Foliage—The leaves on trees and plants.

Germinate—To sprout; to begin growing from a seed.

Greenhouse—A room or building with glass or plastic walls. Plants will grow all year long in a greenhouse.

Humidity—Moisture in the air.

Nightshade—A large family of poisonous and nonpoisonous plants, including the tobaccos, red peppers, tomatoes, potatoes, petunias, and eggplants.

Nutritious—Nourishing; having food value.

Legumes—A plant whose seeds grow in pods, such as peas, beans, lentils, and peanuts.

Oxygen—A gas that has no odor or color. Oxygen makes up about one fifth of the air.

Pinch—Plucking out new growth at the tips of plants to encourage them to branch out and become bushy.

Recycle—To save and use again, perhaps in a new way.

Ritual—The set form for a special ceremony.

Root—The part of the plant that grows down into the earth. Roots hold the plant in place. They also take in water and minerals.

Rootball—The roots of a plant mixed together with soil to form a compact ball.

Root bound—When the roots of a plant grow too large for the planter.

Root vegetables—Carrots, beets, parsnips, radishes, and turnips are root vegetables. People can eat these roots, which store nourishment for the plant.

Seedling—A young plant grown from a seed.

Sprout—To begin to grow. Also, a young shoot growing from a seed.

Top-heavy—When a plant grows too heavy on top to be supported by its container.

Transplant—To take from one place and move to another. When you move a plant from one pot to another it is called transplanting or repotting.

🐛 Further Reading 🐛

Bates, Jeffrey, *Seeds to Plants: Projects With Botany,* (Hands On Science Series), Childrens Press, 1989.

Fell, Derek, *A Kid's First Book of Gardening: Growing Plants Indoors and Out,* Running Press, 1989. (Quill & Trowel Award, Garden Writer's Association of America).

Fell, Derek, *A Kid's First Book of Gardening With Greenhouse and Seeds,* Running Press, 1990.

Huff, Barbara A., *Greening of the City Streets: The Story of Community Gardens,* Clarion Books, 1990.

Jennings, Terry, *Seeds and Seedlings,* (The Young Scientist Investigates Series), Childrens Press, 1989.

Marcus, Elizabeth, *The Amazing World of Plants,* (Troll Question and Answer Books) Troll Associates, 1984.

Markmann, Erika, *Grow It!: An Indoor-Outdoor Gardening Guide for Kids,* Random House Books for Young Readers, 1991.

Raferty, Kevin and Kim G. Raferty, *Kids Gardening: A Kid's Guide to Messing Around in the Dirt,* Klutz Press, 1990. (Includes 15 varieties of seeds)

Robson, Denny, *Grow It for Fun: Hands-on Projects,* Franklin Watts, 1991.

Taylor, Barbara, *Green Thumbs Up!: The Science of Growing Plants,* Random House Books for Young Readers, 1992.

❧ Index ❧